By Faith, I Can

A 21-Day Devotional Journey to Make the Impossible

Possible by Faith

by

Cassandra K. Faire-Cormier

Faire-ing Well Press

Published by Faire-ing Well Press
Houston, TX

Edited by Elizabeth Maynard Charle
Cover design by Cassandra K Faire-Cormier

ISBN: 979-8-9933032-0-8
First edition: October 2025

To every soul who has stood at the edge of doubt and chosen to step forward anyway, this is for you. May you find your faith fierce, your spirit steady, and God ever nearby.

Contents

Preface

You hold in your hands more than a devotional—you hold a declaration. These pages were born in moments of silence, struggle, and surrender. They speak to the one who doesn't need more noise, but who desperately needs more Jesus. If that's you, welcome. You belong here.

This is faith that walks. Faith that weeps. Faith that rises. Each chapter is a rhythm of revelation: a scriptural truth, a spiritual mirror, and a bold declaration. And at the close of each, you'll find a Faith Moment—a space to pause, reflect, and prophesy over your own life.

Faith is not just a concept, it's a lifeline. It's the invisible thread that pulls us forward when everything around us screams, "Stay where you are." It held me in seasons of deep doubt and lifted me in moments of divine clarity. My journey has been a tapestry of valleys and mountaintops, silence and song, but through it all, faith was the one thing I could not afford to relinquish.

Hebrews 11, often referred to as the "Hall of Faith," is not a list of perfect people. It is a lineage of the persistent. Flawed, fragile, yet faithful souls who dared to believe before they saw. Abel, Enoch, Noah, Abraham, and Sarah … each obeyed when they didn't have the full picture. They hoped when it seemed foolish to hope. They trusted when there was no map.

That's the heart of this book.

By Faith, I Can … is more than a phrase, it's a posture. A declaration made in the face of resistance. It's what we whisper through tears, what we shout in triumph, and what we cling to in every uncertain in-between.

Every chapter you're about to read was born in the presence of God, refined through personal struggle, and infused with sacred hope. This isn't just a devotional. It's a journey. A guide. A mirror. A fire-starter.

So, whether your faith feels like a mountain or a small mustard seed, you belong here. You are seen, loved, and equipped by a God who honors faith—even in its trembling form.

As you turn these pages, don't just read, respond. Let the Word stir you. Let each reflection lead you into declaration. And let this truth take root in your soul.

By faith … you can.

The Faith Argument

By Faith, I Can …

The ordinary can be extraordinary, and the impossible can be made possible by faith.

Faith is the confidence that what we hope for will happen; it gives us assurance about things we cannot see (Hebrews 11:1). Faith gives us power, victory, and boldness in that the ordinary can be extraordinary and the impossible can be made possible.

Most likely you have heard those few lines taken from the pages of Scripture about faith. You recall whenever you felt like you were at the end of your rope, you recite, "for we walk by faith, not by sight" (2 Corinthians 5:7 NIV) or, "if you have faith the size of a mustard seed, you will say to this mountain, 'Move from here to there,' and it will move; and nothing will be impossible for you" (Matthew 17:20 NIV). If we need faith, why does Jesus emphasize that even a small amount, the size of a mustard seed, can move mountains? What is the significance of having faith?

First, let us examine what faith really is. Faith by definition is having complete confidence in something or someone. So, let's looks at 2 Corinthians 5:7 again, "for we walk by faith, not by sight" and align with the definition. Taken literally, this means you would have complete confidence in walking where you cannot see. That is kind of scary, is it not?

I recount my mother telling the story of my cousin and me visiting with our grandparents over the summer months when we were three and five years old. We were put to bed around eight thirty in the evening, but at some point, later in the night, we would wake each other up to ask for water. We did not want to alarm the entire house, so we did not turn on any lights. I would take off running in the dark to my grandparents' bedroom, for they were more understanding of us being thirsty than our parents. I never thought about running into anything or knocking any of the precious novelties my grandmother so treasured, off the tables.

On the other hand, my cousin always seemed to have trouble following me, and the sound of crashing glass and porcelain would be left in his wake as he passed through in the dark. One night, as we made our escape to ask for water, my mother followed. She did not follow by walking upright. She decided to get down on all fours and crawl, which was about my height then, to see if there was some glimpse of light at my level, allowing me to confidently move through the dark without incident. She concluded that it was just as dark at my level as it was standing upright.

She asked me, "How do you see where you are going in the dark?"

I replied, "I don't know, Mommy. I just go."

This childhood experience taught me something profound about faith. Reflecting on that time as a child, I realized that faith is not knowing what is in front of you, but moving forward regardless and being confident in your steps.

Now that we know what faith is, let us explore why we have or should have it. The reason we should have it is simple yet somewhat complex. The simple answer is that faith gives us confidence and conviction. We have confidence or the certainty that what we hope for will be realized. We have conviction in that we have a method to counter any doubt.

This brings us to the complex reality of progression, the very thing that makes faith challenging. The complex answer is that having faith initiates the progression toward receiving God's blessings.

Progression is what makes this difficult. Progression is a process, and with any process, there is a course of action or undertaking.

We are reminded in Hebrews 11:6 that "without faith it is impossible to please God," because anyone who comes to Him must believe He exists and rewards those who earnestly seek Him. The progression of our faith is proportionate to the realization of our promises The promises God has for us are tied to how much we believe.

Faith is not soft. It is not merely decorative, reserved for Sunday language or moments of crisis. Faith is an argument, a counter to fear, logic, and what we see with our eyes and feel in our bones.

It argues for the unseen. It pleads the case for hope in the face of despair. Faith doesn't always shout, but it never sits quietly. It contends. It pushes against the grain of circumstance and dares to declare: "This is not the end."

We need faith that fights. Faith that whispers, "I still believe," when everything around us suggests we shouldn't. We need faith that rises in the dark and makes its case even with trembling hands.

That is the heartbeat of this devotional. A faith that isn't always tidy but is always reaching.

Now, let's declare … the following pages aren't just reflections—they are rallying cries. You're not just reading, you are rising.

Day 1
By Faith, I Can Look Forward

"Brothers and sisters, I do not consider myself yet to have taken hold of it. But one thing I do: Forgetting what is behind and straining toward what is ahead, I press on toward the goal to win the prize for which God has called me heavenward in Christ Jesus."
—Philippians 3:13-14 (NIV)

It is easy to reflect on the past and live there. We often find comfort in the past because we are familiar with the joy and pain. But how do we see what is ahead if we are always looking back?

You are absolutely right if you answered you cannot. If you are looking back while moving ahead, you are likely to encounter a grave outcome.

Scripture tells us our future should be founded in your faith. The past is something to look back on; not something to live in. Philippians 3:13-14 reads, "Brothers and sisters, I do not consider myself yet to have taken hold of it. But one thing I do: Forgetting what is behind and straining toward what is ahead, I press on toward the goal to win the prize for which God has called me heavenward in Christ Jesus." In the passage, Paul asserts that forward motion is better than backward reflection.

Yes, we have been hurt, abused, mistreated, or taken advantage of by our loved ones, jobs, and even our churches. However, if we stand there holding on to these painful memories and ideals, we can never realize our future or potential.

There is a story of a lady named Cynthia who had so many successes throughout her lifetime that you would have thought there was nothing she had not attempted with success. She was the best at whatever she decided to do. In high school, she had never played tennis, nor did she know the rules of the game. But one day she decided to try out for the team. Not only did she succeed in making the team, she went on to excel at the sport.

After college, she went on to work in corporate America, rising to the top of the corporate ladder at a record pace, and then left there for a career in sales, where she had absolutely no experience. She somehow excelled in that career as well. Things seemed to have gone well for her, no matter what she decided to do. Most people said she had a natural gift, but one day she struggled with her present situation. She had ended a relationship that left her depleted emotionally, mentally, and financially. When she found herself in the presence of those who appeared to be doing more and appeared to have more, she would recant her past successes and find comfort to escape the harsh realities of the day and what she needed to do to move forward.

Cynthia's story illustrates what Paul understood in Philippians. Sometimes our greatest victories come when we stop rehearsing past success and press forward into new territory. Some key points can be gained from Paul's account in Philippians and from Cynthia's story.

The first of these is the case of premeditated amnesia. Premeditated means intentional, deliberate, and calculated. Premeditated amnesia is the calculated, deliberate intention to forget. If what you remember of your past is damaging enough to hold you back from the future God has for you, then you must intentionally and deliberately forget. You have to find forgiveness and resolve within yourself and act in a way that proves your future expectations outweigh your past limitations.

Another takeaway is to focus on the path forward. There is that old adage, no pain no gain. That saying explicitly applies in this case. Have you ever looked in the mirror and thought to yourself, something has got to change? You then get a gym membership and maybe a personal trainer to assist. About halfway to your goal, you think about how dissatisfied you were before working out, but then you look at how much further you have to go to meet your goals, knowing it is going to require a more intense workout regimen. Although the regimen will be painful and exhausting, you endure the pain to achieve the end result.

Moving on from your past is much like that. Moving forward is not easy, and it will be painful, but hold on to the belief that what is ahead of you is far better than the heartache and frustration of what is behind you.

By faith, you can move forward. God has so much in store for you, but he cannot give you a future if your gaze is set in the past. That would be like God putting you in the driver's seat of a moving car, but instead of looking ahead, you constantly stare in the rearview mirror. That would be a catastrophe waiting to happen, right? Therefore, go for the win by aligning your path to God's will, being the person God has called you to be, and having faith that your move forward will lead to your destiny.

Boldly Declare:

By faith, I release the weight of my past Old wounds will not define me.

My gaze is fixed forward, my stride aligned with God's call.

I choose to press. I will not pause.

What's ahead of me is greater than what's behind me.

By faith, I can move forward.

Faith Moment

- What part of your past are you still rehearsing, and how is it clouding your vision of what God has prepared ahead?
- Ask Him: What must I release to walk fully in what You've promised?
- Write a simple prayer, a bold declaration, or even one sentence that says: I'm moving forward, by faith.

Day 2
By Faith, I Can Rise Again

"Do not gloat over me, my enemy! Though I have fallen, I will rise. Though I sit in darkness, the Lord will be my light."
—Micah 7:8 (NIV)

The enemy wants you to believe that your fall is fatal. That your mistake disqualified you. That your story is over. But the Word of God speaks a better truth: though you have fallen, you will rise.

Peter knew this truth well. The night Jesus was arrested, Peter denied Him not once but three times. And yet, after the resurrection, Jesus didn't rebuke Peter, He restored him (John 21). Three denials met with three affirmations: Do you love Me? Feed My sheep.

Peter's restoration reveals a profound truth about God's character. When placed in God's hands, failure becomes a holy turning point. It's not the end; it's the beginning of a comeback.

Think of a seed buried underground. In the darkness, it looks like death. But what the soil sees as burial, God sees as planting. Your failure is not your funeral, it's your formation.

Joseph was thrown into a pit by his brothers, sold into slavery, falsely accused, and imprisoned. Years passed. Dreams delayed. Promises remained unfulfilled. And yet, when famine came, Joseph was in the perfect position to save nations. What they meant for evil, God meant for good. (Genesis 50:20)

That detour you've had? Divine. That heartbreak you endured? Holy. That closed door? Constructed to redirect you.

Like Joseph, your setback may actually be God's setup. Think of it this way. A slingshot pulls you back before it launches you forward. Every pull, every strain, every moment you feel like you're losing ground is only God getting ready to propel you into purpose.

Faith doesn't ignore the fall, it looks it square in the face and says, "You don't define me."

In Isaiah 61:3, God promises beauty for ashes, the oil of joy for mourning, and a garment of praise for the spirit of despair. God specializes in restoration. And faith is the currency we use to access it.

You don't rise because you feel strong. You rise because He is strong in you. You rise because He called you. You rise because you are not done.

Like a boxer knocked down in the ring, it's not the fall that counts. Rather it's whether you get back up. And faith is your reason to rise.

What failure have you let define you? Where have you assumed it's over when God is still writing? Take time to write a new ending.

Boldly Declare:

By faith, I rise again. My failure is not final. My past has no power. My God restores. I will not sit in shame. I will stand in grace. I will walk in purpose. I will finish what He started in me. In Jesus' name.

You've got breath in your lungs and promise in your soul. So, shake off the dust, silence the shame, and take your next step.

By faith, you can rise again.

Faith Moment

- What situation in your life feels like a fall you can't recover from?
- Write about it honestly. Then ask God to show you what He's restoring in the dark.
- Complete this declaration: *By faith, I rise again because …*
- Let your words become your stand-up moment.

Day 3
By Faith, I Can Wait

"But if we hope for what we do not yet have, we wait for it patiently."
—Romans 8:25 (NIV)

Waiting isn't passive, it's pressure. It's the quiet battlefield between what God promised and when He delivers. It's where faith is tested not by storms, but by silence. But by faith, we don't just endure the wait, we fight the battle well.

The enemy wants us to believe that waiting means nothing is happening. But Heaven doesn't waste time. While we wait, God is working in us, around us, and through us. Waiting is not punishment, it's preparation.

"Let perseverance finish its work so that you may be mature and complete, not lacking anything." (James 1:4)

There's a farmer who plants in the spring, but the harvest doesn't come the next morning. He doesn't dig up the seeds to check on them. Instead, he waters, watches, and works the soil, knowing growth is invisible long before it's visible. The waiting season is part of the harvest season. He doesn't panic. Instead, he prepares.

Faith isn't just about what God will do; it's about who God is. "He has made everything beautiful in its time." (Ecclesiastes 3:11)

Faith believes that God's clock is set to eternal perfection, even when our calendar screams for the breakthrough.

Bitterness makes the wait toxic. Faith makes it holy.

Faith doesn't whine; it worships while it waits. Faith doesn't panic when the answer doesn't come by the deadline. Faith learns to rest even while our trust in God is uncertain. "The Lord is good to those who wait for him, to the soul who seeks him." (Lamentations 3:25)

There's a woman who stood in line for years, applying for jobs and receiving rejection after rejection. Every interview gave her practice and every "no" sharpened her discernment. One day, she walked into a role she never could've handled five years before. The waiting made her wise. If God had answered her earlier prayer, it would've broken her. But He matured her through the wait.

Faith doesn't tiptoe, faith steps bold! It walks forward like the door's already open, like the healing has already happened, and like the chains are already broken; because in the Kingdom of God, it isn't a maybe, it's already done! So don't curse the waiting room. It's the holy place where God stitches strength into your bones. It's where He prepares the path, but more than that, it's where He prepares you.

By faith, you can wait. Not because it's easy. But because God has called you to be faithful. So, worship while you wait. Grow while you wait. And you will stand in expectation, not exhaustion, because delay is still divine when God is the One writing your story!

Boldly Declare:

God, if You've got me in the waiting room, it must be because You're building something I'm not ready to carry yet.

"God, I trust Your timing,.

"I believe You see more than I do. I believe You are good even when it's slow.

"I believe delay is not denial."

"By faith, I can wait on You!"

Faith Moment

- Where are you being asked to wait, even when you'd rather move? What is God developing in you during the delay? Let this be your time to shift from questioning to trusting.
- Complete this declaration: *By faith, I will wait well because …*
- And remember, delay is still divine when God is in it.

Day 4
By Faith, I Can Speak Life

"The tongue has the power of life and death, and those who love it will eat its fruit."
—Proverbs 18:21 (NIV)

Words aren't just sounds; they're seeds. What you say plants either life or decay. Scripture is clear. Our mouths are the gateway to miracles or messes. Life and death are not found in circumstances first, but rather in confessions.

Proverbs 18:21 is not poetic exaggeration; it's spiritual law. Just like gravity holds you to Earth, the principle of your words holds you to outcomes. What you speak today shapes what you walk in tomorrow. In Genesis, God spoke the world into existence. And we, made in His image, carry the echo of that same creative authority.

But here's the question. How do you speak life when you're surrounded by pain? How do you declare joy when depression is louder? How do you bless your future when your present looks like a mess?

Too often, we rehearse defeat. Instead of what God has already declared, we repeat what the enemy says:

"I'm not enough." "Nothing ever changes." "I'll never recover." These aren't just thoughts; they're prophecies we put on repeat.

This principle of speaking life over death isn't just biblical theory; it's witnessed firsthand.

There was a woman who spoke Psalm 91 over her sick husband every day. Doctors gave up, but she didn't. Her words didn't deny reality; they declared God's authority over it. He walked out of that hospital on his own legs, not because of perfect medicine, but because of persistent faith.

Your words are not weak. They are weapons. When fear whispers, "It's over," faith replies, "Not yet." When grief groans, "You're broken," faith rises up and says, "But not beyond repair."

Every time you open your mouth, you choose what kingdom you're partnering with: the one that steals, kills, and destroys, or the one that restores, revives, and resurrects.

So don't just talk about the mountain. Talk to it.

Don't just name the pain. Name the promise.

Don't just echo defeat. Proclaim destiny.

Faith doesn't stutter in the face of the impossible; it shouts anyway! Faith doesn't consult feelings before speaking truth; it declares in spite of them! Faith says, "This body may be breaking, but my spirit is built for battle." Faith says, "My child may be wandering, but I still speak purpose over their life." Faith walks into chaos and says, "Peace, be still!"

Not because of who you are, but because of whose you are. "Let the redeemed of the Lord say so …" (Psalm 107:2 NIV)

So don't let your silence betray your salvation. You are a kingdom speaker. You are an atmosphere shifter. You are the echo of Heaven in a hurting world.

Boldly Declare:

By faith, I will speak life.

My words will not mirror my fear; they will magnify my faith. I declare healing over sickness. Peace over panic. Joy over heaviness. Purpose over the past.

I silence every lie with truth. I cancel every curse with a blessing. I don't wait to feel strong; I speak strength until I stand.

In Jesus' name, I speak life!

Faith Moment

- What have you been speaking over your life, your health, your family, or your future? Are your words echoing fear or faith?

- Take a moment to write one declaration of life, rooted in God's Word, that you will begin speaking daily, no matter what you see: By faith, I declare …

Day 5
By Faith, I Can Love Fully

"Above all, love each other deeply, because love covers over a multitude of sins."
—1 Peter 4:8 (NIV)

L ove is not a suggestion; it is the standard. Peter wrote not about surface-level affection, but about deep, sacrificial, soul-tending love. This is the kind of love that carries others when they can't carry themselves, that prays when offended, and stays rooted when everything else is pulling away.

Peter wrote this letter to believers under persecution. The Roman Empire was cracking down. Christians were being scattered, hunted, and falsely accused. And yet, what did Peter tell them to do? "Love each other deeply."

He didn't say guard your hearts or pull back. He said lean in.

When the world goes dark, love shines brighter. When fear rises, let love rise higher. Peter's instruction wasn't just for the first-century believers facing persecution, it speaks directly to our contemporary struggles with trust and vulnerability.

This wasn't emotional advice. It was spiritual instruction.

Let's be honest: Loving deeply is hard when you've been deeply wounded.

How do you love again after betrayal?

How do you open your heart when it's still bleeding?

How do you stay soft in a world that teaches you to harden?

We live in a time where love is transactional, performative, or withheld. Real love, deep love, requires vulnerability, and vulnerability feels like risk. But faith calls us to something more: it calls us to risk anyway.

Jesus loved Judas. Sat him at the same table. Washed his feet. Called him "friend." Jesus knew Judas would betray Him, and still He loved with full integrity and divine clarity. He didn't love because Judas was trustworthy. He loved because He was love.

A woman in a counseling session once whispered, "I want to forgive, but I don't want to be a fool." She had loved someone who misused her loyalty. She wasn't bitter, but she was bruised. Through prayer, boundaries, and time, she didn't just heal, she learned to love again without losing herself. Because love, when rooted in God, doesn't make you foolish. It makes you free.

Here's the lie: if I love fully, I'll be taken advantage of.

Here's the truth: if I love fully in God, I'll never lose, because I'm anchored in the One who is love itself.

Faith doesn't call us to be naïve. Faith calls us to be courageous. To set boundaries without building walls. To lead with grace, not guardedness. To trust God more than we fear people.

The enemy wants you to believe that love makes you weak. But God says love is your weapon. Love breaks yokes. Love disarms darkness. Love sets captives free, including you.

You have permission to love again!

You don't have to wait until it's safe, until it makes sense, or until they earn it. Love because He first loved you.

Love like it's warfare.

Love like it's strategy.

Love like it's your legacy.

When you love fully, you mirror Christ. You confuse the enemy. You break generational patterns. You speak life into places where silence had suffocated truth.

That heartbreak? Holy.

That closed heart? Opening now.

That love you thought died? God's breathing into it again.

This is not emotional hype, it's spiritual reawakening. By faith, you can love fully.

Boldly Declare:

By faith, I will love fully.

Not out of fear, but out of freedom.

Not because they deserve it, but because I am called to it.

I will love again. I will trust wisely.

I will guard my heart, but not lock it away.

I am healed, whole, and still capable of divine, radical love.

Faith Moment

- Where have you been afraid to love again? Ask God to show you where fear has taken the place of love — in friendships, in family, and even in your self-talk. Take a deep breath. Say, "God, I'm willing." You don't need to have it all figured out — just bring your heart.
- Who needs your forgiveness, even if they never apologize?
- Where is God asking you to love without keeping score?

Day 6
By Faith, I Can Lead

"Have I not commanded you? Be strong and courageous. Do not be afraid; do not be discouraged, for the Lord your God will be with you wherever you go."

—Joshua 1:9 (NIV)

Leadership is not about status, it's about surrender. When God called Joshua to lead after Moses, He didn't give him a plan. He gave him a promise: "I will be with you."

God doesn't call the fearless. He calls the faithful. Joshua had watched Moses carry the people for forty years. He knew the burden. He saw the cost. And now that same mantle was resting on his shoulders. But God didn't say, "You better live up to Moses."

God said, "Be strong and courageous … for I am with you."

This was not just a pep talk; it was a divine charge. Because leading in the name of God requires courage that doesn't come from confidence, but from communion.

If you've ever been called to lead, at home, in ministry, or on the job, you know the feeling:

"Who am I to do this?"

"What if I fail?"

"What if they don't follow?"

Fear whispers sabotage. It questions timing. It tries to cloak leadership in imposter syndrome and delay. But faith? Faith silences fear by walking forward anyway.

I once watched a young woman rise to lead a nonprofit rooted in justice. She was doubted, second-guessed, and dismissed. But she stayed the course. She prayed. She planned. And she produced fruit that silenced every critic. Not by shouting, but by standing. By staying.

The lie says: You're not ready.

The truth says: God is already ahead of you.

You don't need all the answers to lead. You need the anointing to obey.

Faithful leadership doesn't mean knowing everything. It means trusting the One who does.

God's not asking you to feel brave. He's asking you to show up anyway.

Now hear this in your spirit: "You don't have to wait for fear to leave. Lead anyway. Speak anyway. Stand anyway."

Your "yes" is the gateway for someone else's breakthrough.

Your obedience breaks chains you can't even see.

The enemy wants to paralyze your potential. But God? He's pushing you to lead like you were born for it, because you were.

And if you tremble? Tremble with purpose. Tremble and lead anyway.

Boldly Declare:

By faith, I will lead without fear.

I am not perfect, but I am positioned.

I don't need full clarity to walk in full calling.

God goes before me. God strengthens me.

By faith, I will not shrink.

I will rise and lead.

Faith Moment

- Take a moment and sit with God. Ask Him to show you the dreams He's still breathing on. Is there a vision you've set aside because you didn't feel ready—or worthy?

- Write it down again. Let this be your quiet "yes." You don't need to know how. You just need to believe it's possible again.

- What dream is God inviting you to resurrect in this season?

- What's one step of faith you can take this week to move toward it?

Day 7
By Faith, I Can Remember

"Can a woman forget her nursing child, or show no compassion for the child of her womb? Even these may forget, yet I will not forget you. See, I have inscribed you on the palms of My hands."
—Isaiah 49:15-16 (NRSV)

These words in Isaiah address a specific kind of pain, the ache of feeling forgotten. There is a kind of loneliness that doesn't come from being alone—it comes from feeling unseen. Overlooked. Set aside. Forgotten. You may be surrounded by people yet still carry the ache of invisibility, wondering if your prayers slipped into God's voicemail, if Heaven placed you on hold.

But hear this: God has not forgotten you. Before you were formed, He knew you. And not just the version that has it all together—but the you who cries in the bathroom, the you who's weary of waiting, and the you who keeps showing up even when it hurts. The world may scroll past you, but Heaven never does.

God has inscribed your name on His hands—not in pencil, not with ink—but engraved with the permanence of love that doesn't fade or change its mind. You are remembered. Not generally, but intimately. Not as a number, but as a name. His silence is not absence. His delay is not neglect. His timing is not rejection. What feels like being forgotten is often the sacred pause before your unfolding.

There was a woman who served quietly for years in her church. No titles. No spotlight. Just faithfulness. She cleaned the sanctuary, prayed for strangers, and gave generously from what little she had. One Sunday, the pastor called her forward. She assumed she was being asked to assist with communion—but instead, she was honored before the whole congregation.

Tears filled her eyes—not because of the applause, but because she finally felt seen. But here's the truth: God had seen her all along. Even when no one else had.

Boldly Declare:

I am not invisible.

I am not overlooked.

I am not the one God skipped over when He was handing out purpose.

By faith, I am not forgotten—I am remembered in detail.

My name is etched on His palm.

My tears are caught in His bottle.

My prayers didn't vanish into the void—they were planted, and now they rise.

He saw me in the dark before I ever stood in the light.

He called me before I knew how to answer.

He kept me when I didn't know I was being kept.

I am not forgotten. I am marked. I am known. I am chosen. He prepares a table in full view of what tried to erase me. And every delay? Just divine staging for the glory about to break. So, I lift my head, square my shoulders, and walk into the room like one Heaven remembers.

By faith—I declare: I am not forgotten. I am seen. I am sent. I am sacred.

Faith Moment

- Take a quiet breath. Close your eyes. Whisper your name aloud and imagine it glowing—written on the hand of God. Now ask Him to help you walk in the confidence of someone fully remembered. Because you are.

Day 8
By Faith, I Can Move Mountains

"For truly I tell you, if you have faith the size of a mustard seed, you will say to this mountain, 'Move from here to there,' and it will move. Nothing will be impossible for you."
—Matthew 17:20 (CSB)

Faith isn't measured in weight but in where it rests. Jesus wasn't talking about quantity; He was pointing to trust. Even the smallest belief in a limitless God can overthrow the tallest obstacle. This isn't about hype; it's about alignment.

As Jesus descended from a moment of divine glory on the mountain, He was met with chaos. A man's son was in crisis, possessed and tormented, and the disciples failed to bring relief. They had been given authority, but something wasn't working. They missed the activation of faith.

Jesus stepped in, rebuked the spirit, and the boy was set free. Later, the disciples asked what went wrong. His answer cut through the confusion: "You didn't believe enough." And then He revealed a staggering truth—even faith as small as a mustard seed carries power to relocate mountains.

He wasn't being poetic. He was being precise.

We all face what feels immovable. For some, it's the weight of financial uncertainty. For others, it's chronic illness, fractured relationships, or internal battles that no one sees. These aren't symbolic issues. They are real, they are heavy, and they don't budge easily.

And if we're honest, we've all wondered: Is my faith not enough? Why won't this thing change? Why does breakthrough come for others while I stay stuck?

A woman I know was days from losing her home. Jobless. Out of savings. She didn't beg; she stood. Every morning, she touched the walls of her house and thanked God for provision she hadn't seen yet. Just before her move-out date, she was hired into a position that paid more than any role she'd ever had. Her situation didn't shift because she panicked. It changed because she stood firm.

Doubt wants to keep your eyes on the size of the problem. But the truth is, it's not about being flawless in your belief, it's about surrendering what little trust you do have to a God who never fails.

You don't need to fake strength. You don't have to pretend it's easy. But you do need to plant your faith, even if it feels fragile, in the One who always keeps His word.

Faith doesn't apologize for showing up. Faith doesn't play it safe. Faith doesn't knock. Instead, it enters.

Faith speaks up when fear tries to silence. Faith addresses the sickness. Faith confronts the addiction. Faith speaks to the chaos and says, "You don't get the final word."

The same God who tore down Jericho's walls, who opened prison doors for Paul and Silas, who fed thousands with a boy's lunch, He's still active, still present, and He's on your side.

So don't just think about the problem. Talk back to it. Stand in your authority. Claim the promise.

Boldly Declare:

I trust God to do what I can't. I will no longer shrink when faced with opposition. I will speak with confidence, move with courage, and rest in the knowledge that my belief, even when it feels small, is enough to unlock Heaven's response.

Yes, the obstacle is real. But my God is greater.

I'm not waiting on the mountain to move. I'm commanding it, and it's shifting now.

Faith Moment

- What mountain have you been staring at in silence? Where have you hesitated to speak because your faith felt too small?

- Write the name of your mountain, then write a declaration to it. Let your mustard-seed faith speak. *By faith, I declare …*

Day 9
By Faith, I Can Heal

"He heals the brokenhearted and binds up their wounds."
—Psalm 147:3 (NIV)

Faith is what keeps us walking when pain tells us to quit. You don't have to be unscarred to be whole. You just have to trust the One who knows how to turn wounds into witnesses.

Psalm 147 speaks of a God who rebuilds, restores, and heals. He gathers the exiles, lifts the humble, and pours out rain on dry places. But right in the middle of these grand moves, the psalmist makes it personal: "He heals the brokenhearted." That's not poetic, it's personal.

This verse isn't about physical strength or surface comfort. It's about the God who enters the raw, torn places in our lives and wraps them with grace—the One who doesn't rush our pain but walks with us through it.

We're all carrying something. Maybe it's a body that won't cooperate. Maybe it's a heart crushed by betrayal. Maybe it's trauma that keeps replaying no matter how much time has passed.

And while people say, "Just get over it," faith says, "Bring it to God." Because healing isn't about ignoring pain, it's about inviting God into it.

We cry. We question. We break. But by faith, we also heal.

The woman with the issue of blood, in Mark 5, had suffered for twelve years. Doctors had drained her financially, and still, her condition worsened. But one day, she reached out. She didn't ask permission. She didn't make a scene. She just touched the edge of Jesus' garment, and immediately, healing came.

It wasn't the crowd. It wasn't the robe. It was her faith that made her whole.

I knew a man whose grief after losing his child nearly swallowed him. He stopped attending church and stopped praying. But one day, while watching an old sermon online, he started to weep, not from sadness, but from release. That was the beginning of his healing. He didn't heal in a day, but that day, healing started. And that's what faith does. It starts something new, even when the old still hurts.

Pain says, "This will always be who you are."

Faith says, "This is what God is healing in you."

Pain wants to freeze you. Faith invites you to move, even if it's limping.

You are not your wound. You are not your diagnosis. You are not the sum of what happened to you.

You are becoming something new, and faith is how you participate in that transformation.

Faith doesn't ignore the pain; it partners with the Healer.

Faith says, "Even if I still feel it, I trust You're working on it."

Faith goes to therapy and church. Faith prays and processes. Faith holds space for miracles and medicine.

The same God who raised Lazarus …Who touched lepers …Who told the lame man, "Take up your mat and walk," is the same God working in you.

He heals broken hearts, wounded bodies, and weary souls. And no matter how long it's been, healing is still possible.

Boldly Declare:

By faith, I believe healing is my portion.

I refuse to settle for numbness or bitterness.

I will not be defined by pain. Instead, I will walk in the power of God's restoration.

I release what I can't fix. I trust the God who can.

My story doesn't end with the wound; it continues with healing.

By faith, I can heal.

Faith Moment

- What wound have you been carrying that needs the touch of the Healer? Where have you settled for survival when God is calling you to wholeness?
- Name what you're releasing. *By faith, I release ...*
- Write what you're believing. *By faith, I receive healing in ...*

Day 10
By Faith, I Can Finish Strong

"I have fought the good fight, I have finished the race, I have kept the faith."

—2 Timothy 4:7 (NIV)

Finishing strong isn't about how fast you ran. It's about the faith you carried, the endurance you built, and the legacy you leave. Faith is the fuel that turns weariness into witness.

In Paul's letter, he didn't list his accomplishments. He didn't brag about the churches he planted or the sermons he preached. He simply declared: "I finished."

Historically, this was Paul's farewell. Spiritually, it's a challenge to every believer: the race matters, but so does the finish.

You've started things with fire before, only to see them fade. You've grown tired in the waiting, discouraged by delay. You've questioned if you'll ever complete what you began.

But faith says finishing is still possible, even if you're limping toward the line. Even if your journey looks different than others.

A mother went back to school in her fifties after raising five children. She graduated with honors. Her degree wasn't just a piece of paper; it was proof that endurance pays off.

You're not too late. The delay was preparation, not punishment.

God doesn't anoint you to burn out. He anoints you to break through.

Your faith is not wasted. Your obedience is not overlooked. You're not just finishing for yourself; you're finishing for the ones who will follow.

Finish strong! Run with your eyes fixed on the Author and Finisher. Walk when you can't run. Crawl if you must. But don't stop.

Heaven is cheering you on. The cloud of witnesses is watching. Your legacy is still being written.

This isn't the end. This is the exclamation mark!

Boldly Declare:

By faith, I will finish strong. My endurance is rising. My purpose is clear. My legacy is holy.

I will not quit. I will not coast. I will complete what God began in me.

By faith, the finish is just the beginning.

Faith Moment

- Where have you been tempted to stop short? What unfinished purpose is God calling you to complete?
- Write down the assignment you're committing to finish, not in your own strength, but by His Spirit. *By faith, I will finish …*
- Write down areas in your life you will not give up on, not in your own strength, but by the power of the Holy Spirit. *By faith, I will not give up on …*

Day 11
By Faith, I Can Build Again

"They will rebuild the ancient ruins and restore the places long devastated; they will renew the ruined cities that have been devastated for generations."
—Isaiah 61:4 (NIV)

God doesn't just rescue, He restores. He doesn't simply lift you up, He positions you to rebuild. Faith doesn't stop at survival; it compels you to gather the bricks of what was broken and begin again, bolder and better.

Isaiah 61 speaks prophetically of healing and restoration. The ruins in this passage are generational, structural, and spiritual. Yet, God commissions the very people who were once broken to become the builders of hope.

Historically, this promise was to the exiles of Israel. Spiritually, it is for every person who looks at the debris of their life and wonders, "Can anything rise from this again?"

You've been through the storm, and you survived. But now you look at the pieces, unsure if you have the strength to begin again. The grief is heavy. The trauma lingers. The enemy whispers, "Why bother?"

Faith doesn't deny the ruins. It chooses to believe that God still builds masterpieces from ashes. This promise found its embodiment in leaders like Nehemiah, who understood that rebuilding requires both vision and courage.

Nehemiah rebuilt the wall of Jerusalem with a sword in one hand and a tool in the other. He faced mockers, threats, and internal fear, but he built anyway.

A woman who lost everything in a divorce begins to dream again. One step at a time, she starts a business, writes a book, and restores her confidence. Her new life isn't a repeat, it's a resurrection.

The ruins are not your end. They are your blueprint.

That broken relationship? Material for wisdom. That lost opportunity? A foundation for the new. That past mistake? Cemented into the testimony.

Faith isn't about pretending the loss didn't happen. It's about trusting that God can use all of it.

Build again, beloved! Lay brick on brick with holy intention. Pick up your hammer and your hope.

The ruins are being repurposed. The tears are turning into mortar. The laughter will echo through new halls.

Your hands are not too tired. Your dream is not too dead. Your faith is not too small.

God is the Architect. You are the builder. And the blueprint? Already blessed.

Boldly Declare:

By faith, I will build again. Not in my strength, but by His Spirit. Not as I was, but as I am now becoming.

The ruins will rise. The ashes will testify. The dream will live.

By faith, the rebuild begins.

Faith Moment

- What is God calling you to rebuild? What ruins, physical, emotional, or spiritual, is He asking you to reclaim?
- Write a declaration over your restoration journey:
  - *By faith, I will pick up the pieces of …*
  - *By faith, I am rebuilding …*
- Let this be your blueprint prayer. Say it. Speak it. Build it.

Day 12
By Faith, I Can Reclaim My Voice

"Then the Lord reached out His hand and touched my mouth and said to me, 'I have put my words in your mouth.'"
—Jeremiah 1:9 (NIV)

Your voice is not just a sound. It is a sacred instrument, shaped by Heaven and assigned to declare, confront, heal, and build. When God calls, He equips. When He anoints, He appoints. And when He touches your mouth, every silencing lie loses power.

In Jeremiah 1, we meet a young man gripped by insecurity. Called as a prophet to nations, Jeremiah's first instinct was resistance: "I do not know how to speak; I am too young." But God didn't entertain excuses. Instead, He touched Jeremiah's mouth and placed divine words within it. Historically, this moment launched one of Israel's most powerful prophetic voices, not because Jeremiah was bold, but because God was.

Jeremiah's calling wasn't about being eloquent. It was about being obedient. His voice didn't rise from confidence; it rose from consecration. That's the power of a God-ordained voice.

Maybe you've been told you're too loud, too sensitive, or too much. Maybe your silence was survival. Maybe your voice was muted by trauma, religion, culture, or shame. You started believing that quiet was safer than truth, that whispering was holier than testifying.

And so, the enemy exploited the hush. He convinced you your voice wasn't needed. That it wouldn't matter. But Heaven disagrees.

Moses, like Jeremiah, questioned his qualifications: "I am slow of speech and tongue." And yet, through trembling lips, God delivered a nation.

A woman, silenced by years of emotional abuse, finally spoke her truth in a courtroom. Her voice quivered, but it didn't fail. That single act of courage inspired dozens of other women to come forward. Her voice became a door for others to walk through.

Voices reclaimed are never just personal. They are prophetic.

The enemy calls it rebellion. God calls it release.

The world may say you're too loud, but Heaven say you're right on time. Your voice carries healing. It breaks generational curses. It affirms identities. It rewrites stories.

You are not too much. You are appointed.

This isn't about volume. It's about authority. And faith gives you both.

Let the silence be shattered by sacred sound! Let your whisper turn into a war cry!

You will no longer edit your testimony to make others comfortable. You will no longer bow your head when you were made to speak truth.

You are Heaven's echo in the earth!

Your voice will shake rooms, rewrite laws, rebuild families, and revive dry places. When you speak, the kingdom moves.

Because when God says, "I have put my words in your mouth," hell cannot mute you.

Speak, prophet. Roar, daughter. Declare, son. Reclaim what was always yours.

Boldly Declare:

By faith, I reclaim my voice. Not to wound, but to witness. Not to dominate, but to declare. Not to echo fear, but to speak life.

I am not silent. I am not small. I am anointed.

By faith, my voice rises, and it will not be silenced again.

Faith Moment

- What truth have you been afraid to speak? What moment silenced your voice, and what new truth is God asking you to declare today?
- Finish this prompt in your own words:
  - *By faith, I will no longer remain silent about …*
  - *God has given me a voice to …*
  - *Today, I speak life over …*
- Your voice is your testimony. Let this be your declaration of release.

Day 13
By Faith, I Can Live Free

"It is for freedom that Christ has set us free. Stand firm, then, and do not let yourselves be burdened again by a yoke of slavery."
 —Galatians 5:1 (NIV)

Freedom isn't earned. It is gifted by grace, sealed by the cross, and maintained by faith. Jesus didn't die so we could manage our chains. He died to break them completely. Faith gives us permission to step out of prisons we got used to living in.

Paul's letter to the Galatians is a declaration of spiritual independence. The early church was caught in a tug-of-war between the law and grace. Paul reminded them that faith in Christ means freedom from performance-based religion. The gospel wasn't about striving. It was about standing.

Historically, this call to stand firm was a rally cry against returning to old systems. Spiritually, it is still our call: don't go back to what God delivered you from.

You got free, but you didn't stay free. You let guilt become your compass. You let comfort pull you back into habits that kept you bound. You mistook control for peace, and the weight returned.

Freedom feels foreign when you've lived in bondage too long. But faith says: just because it feels unfamiliar, doesn't mean it's not yours.

The Israelites were delivered from Egypt, but they longed for the familiarity of slavery. They had freedom in their hands but bondage in their hearts.

Freedom is a mindset long before it becomes a lifestyle. Your thoughts must be liberated before your circumstances can change. You have to believe you deserve better, that change is possible, and God has more for you, long before you see evidence of it.

A man finally left an unhealthy relationship. For months, he felt unworthy of healthy love. Until one day, he chose to believe that freedom wasn't just about escape, it was about elevation.

You don't owe your chains anything. Not your loyalty. Not your nostalgia. Not your regret.

You are not bound by what happened to you. You are not defined by your weakest moment. God doesn't just want you free from sin, He wants you free from shame.

Faith doesn't manage brokenness. It heals it.

Live free, beloved! Free from comparison. Free from toxic expectations. Free from generational patterns.

Let the world wonder how you broke through. Let them watch you walk out what tried to bury you.

Your past doesn't own your next. Your trauma doesn't own your trust. Your pain doesn't own your praise.

You are the evidence that God still sets captives free!

Boldly Declare:

By faith, I live free. Free from guilt. Free from fear. Free from performance.

I am not tethered to what was. I am anchored in who He is.

By faith, I will not return to my chains. By grace, I will dance in my freedom.

Faith Moment

- Where have you settled for surviving instead of truly living free? What mindset, memory, or habit are you ready to release?
- Write your declaration of liberty:
  - *By faith, I let go of…*
  - *I no longer serve…*
  - *From this day forward, I choose to live free in…*
- Let this be your stand, bold, unburdened, and fully alive in grace.

Day 14
By Faith, I Can Choose

"You did not choose me, but I chose you and appointed you so that you might go and bear fruit—fruit that will last…"
—John 15:16 (NIV)

Being chosen isn't just about favor—it's about divine appointment. God isn't scrambling to find someone; He already placed His hand on you before you were formed in your mother's womb. You didn't earn this calling, and you can't be disqualified by opinions or setbacks. In the heavenly record, your name has already been spoken.

To be chosen means you are not an afterthought. You are not filler. You are called, seen, and sent. Your story, your scars, and your very breath—all part of the calling. You are not tolerated; you are treasured.

A young woman once applied to her dream university—her backup plan already in place because she didn't think she was good enough. But then, the letter arrived: "Congratulations. You've been accepted." No interview, no essay. Her qualifications had already been reviewed, and her name was on the acceptance list before she ever expected it. Sometimes we walk through life believing we are waiting to be picked, but Heaven already stamped "approved" over our name.

Boldly Declare:

I'm not standing here by chance—I was chosen on purpose, with purpose, for purpose. Before I had a name, He gave me an assignment. Before I saw the battle, He crowned me with victory.

I am not overlooked. I am not optional. I am not the backup plan.

I am Heaven's yes in a world full of maybes.

Every rejection was redirection. Every closed door was a corridor to destiny.

Hell had a plan—but God had a promise.

By faith, I rise like I know I'm chosen. I speak like oil is dripping from my lips. I move like angels have cleared the path ahead of me. I no longer audition for approval—I already have the part.

Chosen. Called. Carried. Commissioned.

By faith, I am chosen. And I'll never shrink to fit into a room that was too small for my assignment anyway.

Faith Moment

- Write down three moments in your life when you felt overlooked or rejected.

- Now, beside each, declare aloud: "Today, I choose." Let that truth sink into the bones. You were never forgotten. You were always being positioned.

Day 15
By Faith, I Can Be Secure

"The name of the Lord is a strong tower; the righteous run into it and are safe."

—Proverbs 18:10 (NIV)

Security isn't found in a salary, a title, or the strength of your own hands. True security is anchored in the unshakable character of God. When the winds of uncertainty howl and the world shakes beneath your feet, there is a refuge—a place where fear cannot enter and anxiety must bow. That place is the presence of the Most High.

God is not surprised by your struggles. He's not thrown off by the storms. He is the Strong Tower—ancient, unshakable, built on bedrock that goes deeper than any foundation man can lay—the kind of fortress that has weathered every assault and still stands. You don't have to reinforce your own defenses when God Himself is your stronghold. Within His walls, you find not just protection, but perfect peace. And when the enemy comes for your mind, your joy, and your future—God says, "This one is Mine. Off limits."

I remember a season when everything that made me feel "secure" started to unravel. The job I thought I'd never lose was gone. The people I depended on grew silent. My savings account echoed back nothing but emptiness. I had nothing left to lean on—except Him.

And in that quiet space where I couldn't "do" or "fix" anything, I discovered something more powerful: I was held. Kept. Secure—not because I had it all together, but because He never let go. That kind of security can't be bought. It has to be believed. It's knowing that even if everything else collapses, you are still standing—because you're not standing alone.

Boldly Declare:

I am not fragile—I am fortified.

I don't live on edge—I live in the shadow of the Almighty.

I don't flinch when fear knocks, because I am secure in a God who never fails.

Every lie that told me I was unprotected, exposed, or unseen? Canceled. Dismantled. Done.

I am secure in my identity—no imposter syndrome here.

I am secure in my calling—hell can't revoke what Heaven has assigned.

I am secure in my God—who fights for me, shields me, and walks beside me.

I wear peace like armor. I sleep like still waters.

No weapon formed will ever find its mark— because I am kept, covered, and called.

By faith, I am not just standing. I am standing strong. I am secure.

Faith Moment

- Take a deep breath. Imagine yourself standing in a strong tower overlooking every fear, doubt, and enemy. What does God whisper to you in that place of peace? Write it down.
- Now, hold onto it. Let it be your anchor when the wind rises again.

Day 16
By Faith, I Can Break Chains

"Forget the former things; do not dwell on the past. See, I am doing a new thing! Now it springs up; do you not perceive it?"
—Isaiah 43:18–19 (NIV)

Cycles are patterns that repeat—habits, dysfunctions, and generational mindsets that try to keep us locked in familiar prisons. You may have inherited pain, disappointment, scarcity, or silence. But God is not obligated to repeat what broke you—He is committed to restoring what He destined for you.

When the Spirit of God breathes into your life, old cycles begin to lose their grip. What held your mother, what stifled your father, and what chased your bloodline ends with you. Because faith isn't passive; it's a divine sledgehammer breaking every stronghold that dared to name itself permanent. Breaking cycles requires both recognition and intentional action.

There is a story about a young woman who noticed every woman in her family married an addict. She grew up thinking love had to hurt. But one day, she stood in front of the mirror and said, "I may come from brokenness, but I am not bound to it." She sought God.

She went to counseling. She changed the script. She married differently and raised her children differently, and her legacy is a testimony that faith, when activated, breaks chains.

Boldly Declare:

By faith, I declare the cycles end with me.

I will not live rehearsing my family's pain.

I am not the product of my trauma—I am the evidence of my God.

The curse breaks because I believe.

The patterns stop because I chose differently.

What gripped generations before me will bow to the bloodline of Christ in me.

By faith, I rise, I walk free, and I build anew.

I am a cycle breaker, a legacy maker, and a fire starter.

I am not who I was—I am who He's called me to be.

I am breaking cycles.

Faith Moment

- Take a moment and list any cycles—emotional, relational, financial, or spiritual—you feel the Lord highlighting. Write them down and then draw a line through each one. As you do, speak aloud, "This ends with me. By faith, I choose freedom."

Day 17
By Faith, I Can Be Free of Fear

"For God has not given us a spirit of fear, but of power and of love and of a sound mind."
—2 Timothy 1:7 (NKJV)

Fear is a liar. It whispers of what might go wrong, what you'll lose, and how you'll fail. But fear has no creative power—it can only paralyze. Faith, however, is active. Faith moves. Faith climbs out of the boat when the storm still rages and walks toward the One who commands the waves.

The spirit of fear doesn't come from God. What He gives is power to overcome, love to cast out fear, and a mind that is clear, sound, and rooted in truth. You are not at the mercy of fear—you are anointed to confront it.

A man had a dream to open a business but hesitated for years. Every time he made progress, fear told him, "You're not ready. What if you fail?" One day, he opened his Bible and read 2 Timothy 1:7 like it was the first time. He prayed, took a deep breath, and launched. Now he teaches others how to step out in boldness. Faith didn't erase his fear—it overruled it.

Boldly Declare:

By faith, I reject fear and every lie it rode in on.

I am not small. I am not unworthy. I am not alone.

I have power—God-given power—to speak, move, and rise.

I have love—perfect, fear-casting love.

I have a sound mind—anchored in peace, ordered by truth, and guarded by grace.

Fear is no longer my language.

Anxiety is not my identity.

Doubt cannot sit at my table.

I walk in the freedom of faith.

By faith, I am free from fear.

Faith Moment

- Close your eyes and envision fear as a shadowy figure trying to whisper in your ear.
- Now envision the light of God flooding in—bright, strong, and undeniable. The shadow shrinks and vanishes. Say out loud, "I choose light. I choose truth. I choose freedom."

Day 18
By Faith, I Can Elevate

"Humble yourselves, therefore, under God's mighty hand, that He may lift you up in due time."
—1 Peter 5:6 (NIV)

When God elevates, He doesn't just move you up; He moves you into purpose. But elevation in the kingdom always follows humility. The world says climb your way up. God says bow your heart low. The path to the top in the Spirit is found in surrender.

Sometimes it feels like you're hidden, overlooked, and forgotten. But God sees. He knows how you've served in secret, prayed when no one clapped, remained faithful when others quit. And in His divine time, not a moment too early or too late—He will lift you.

What does this elevation actually look like? It might be the promotion that comes after years of integrity when others were cutting corners. It's the opportunity to speak at the conference after seasons of serving behind the scenes. It's being asked to lead the project because people have watched your character, not just your competence. It's the door that opens not because you networked your way in, but because your faithfulness created a reputation that preceded you.

Think of Joseph. Betrayed by brothers, enslaved, falsely accused, and forgotten in prison. But he never lost faith. In one day, God elevated him from the prison to the palace—not because of ambition, but because of alignment. He wasn't chasing a title. He was stewarding the dream. His elevation looked like this: Pharaoh's desperate need met Joseph's divine preparation. The skills he'd developed managing Potiphar's house prepared him to manage a nation. The wisdom he'd gained in hardship equipped him to navigate abundance.

God's elevation often means you're given influence you didn't campaign for, resources you didn't manipulate to get, and platforms you didn't build for yourself. You find yourself in rooms you never applied to enter, solving problems bigger than your own, affecting lives beyond your immediate circle.

Elevation isn't earned—it's entrusted.

Boldly Declare:

By faith, I believe God is lifting me. I may have been in a season of obscurity, but I am not unseen. I don't have to force my way into rooms—God has already opened the door.

He is raising me to places my resume can't explain. My character is catching up with my calling. I've bowed low, and now God says, "Rise."

I am seated in heavenly places. I walk in authority.

By faith, I am elevated—not to boast, but to bless.

Not to compete, but to consecrate.

Not for applause, but for assignment.

I am elevated by the hand of God.

Faith Moment

- Close your eyes and imagine the hand of God lifting you from your current position. Feel the weight of striving fall off. Whisper, "I trust Your timing, God. I surrender to Your elevation."

Day 19
By Faith, I Can Keep My Peace

"Now to Him who is able to keep you from stumbling and to present you blameless before the presence of His glory with great joy…"
—Jude 1:24 (ESV)

To be kept by God is more than just being protected—it is to be preserved, upheld, and sustained by the One who never sleeps nor slumbers. The Greek word for "keep" here implies continuous guardianship. God isn't reacting to your crises; He's already standing watch, already ensuring your steps align with His divine plan.

There will be moments when your emotions falter, when your resources dwindle, and when the pressure tries to shake you loose—but even in those moments, God's keeping power is not compromised. You don't keep yourself—He keeps you. His Spirit surrounds you like a fortress, and His faithfulness is your shield.

I think of the lighthouse on a stormy coast. Ships may toss and turn in violent waves, but the light never goes out. Its foundation is unshaken, and it continues to shine, keeping sailors on course—even when they can't see the land ahead. That's what it feels like to be kept by God. You may be in the storm, but you're never lost in it. His presence is your light, and His will is your anchor.

Boldly Declare:

I am not slipping. I am not sinking. I am kept. Kept by the hand that flung the stars into the sky. Kept by the One who counted every tear and still called me whole. I do not keep myself together—He keeps me in perfect peace. The chaos around me does not define the calm within me. Hell may strategize, but Heaven secures.

I am held when I don't feel strong.

I am carried when I don't know the way.

I am covered when I can't see what's next.

By faith, I declare: I am not barely surviving—I am divinely sustained.

I am kept for purpose, for glory, for such a time as this.

I will not fall. I will not faint.

Because He who keeps Israel neither slumbers nor sleeps—and He's keeping me.

By faith … I am kept.

Faith Moment

- Take a deep breath and speak this over yourself today: "God, You are my Keeper. You know my going out and my coming in. I rest in Your sovereignty. I release the fear of falling and trust that You've already covered every step ahead."

Day 20
By Faith, I Can Be Enough

"But he said to me, 'My grace is sufficient for you, for my power is made perfect in weakness.' Therefore I will boast all the more gladly about my weaknesses, so that Christ's power may rest on me."
—2 Corinthians 12:9 (NIV)

We live in a world that constantly whispers, "You're not enough." Not talented enough. Not smart enough. Not spiritual enough. But Heaven never said that. God's Word affirms again and again: You are fearfully and wonderfully made. You are the handiwork of the Creator, crafted with intentionality and marked by divine purpose.

Paul didn't boast in having it all together—he boasted in his weakness because it was there that God's strength showed up with power. The world might see your limitations as liabilities, but God sees them as holy openings for His grace to flood in. You don't have to earn the love of God. You don't have to hustle for your worth. You don't have to become someone else to be seen, chosen, or called.

God calls us to grow, to develop our gifts, and to pursue excellence. The key is understanding the difference between healthy striving and soul-crushing hustle. Godly ambition asks, "How can I steward what You've given me for Your glory?" Worldly ambition demands, "How can I prove I'm worthy through what I achieve?"

Healthy striving flows from identity—knowing who you are in Christ fuels what you do for Christ. Unhealthy striving seeks identity—believing that what you accomplish determines your worth. One is rooted in rest; the other is rooted in restlessness.

How can you tell the difference? Godly ambition brings peace even in the process. You can work hard without being anxious, pursue goals without being consumed, and accept delays without being devastated. Worldly ambition leaves you empty even when you succeed, always needing the next achievement to feel valuable.

There was a woman who always felt behind. She compared herself to others who seemed more accomplished, more confident, more everything. For years, she worked seventy-hour weeks, earned advanced degrees, and climbed corporate ladders—but the validation never lasted. Each promotion only revealed how much further she had to climb. One day, exhausted and spiritually bankrupt, she collapsed in prayer and asked God, "What more do I have to become?"

She heard the Spirit whisper, "You don't have to become what you already are." That moment shifted everything. Here's what her transformation looked like: She didn't quit her job, but she stopped working from desperation. She still pursued excellence, but from a place of stewardship rather than survival. She set boundaries, said no to opportunities that didn't align with her calling, and began to measure success by faithfulness rather than just results. Her productivity actually increased because her motivation had been purified.

Her life didn't get easier, but it got fuller. She began to lead from a place of authenticity, parent with confidence, and love without fear of rejection. She found peace not by achieving, but by receiving her identity in Christ.

God's grace covers every gap, and His power lifts every deficit. Your imperfections don't disqualify you— they qualify you for glory. By faith, you don't need to strive to prove you're "enough." You need to believe you already are enough through Christ, then work from that security rather than for it.

Boldly Declare:

I silence the voices of lack, the echoes of unworthiness, and the lies of not enough. I was never meant to measure myself by man's standards—I was marked by God before time began. By faith, I declare: I am not missing anything. I am not a mistake. I am not too late.

I am chosen, equipped, and crowned with purpose.

I am anointed in the cracks, powerful in the process, and radiant in my realness.

I do not shrink. I do not strive—I stand.

By faith, I am enough. And that is more than enough.

Faith Moment

- Take a moment right now and write down five areas where you've questioned your "enough-ness." Beside each one, write what God says about it. Declare aloud: I am not defined by my doubts. I am enough because Christ in me is more than enough.

Day 21
By Faith, I Can Dream Again

"Write the vision and make it plain on tablets, that he may run who reads it. For the vision is yet for an appointed time; but at the end it will speak, and it will not lie. Though it tarries, wait for it; because it will surely come."
—Habakkuk 2:2-3 (NKJV)

Dreams don't die from delay—they die from doubt. The enemy's greatest weapon against your future isn't opposition; it's the whisper that says, "It's too late. You're too old. You've been disappointed too many times." But God doesn't operate on expiration dates. His vision for your life doesn't have a statute of limitations.

Habakkuk received this word during one of Israel's darkest seasons. Injustice was rampant. God seemed silent. The prophet questioned why the righteous suffered while the wicked prospered. Yet in the midst of his complaints, God gave him something to write down—a vision that would outlast the present chaos.

The Hebrew word for "vision" here is *chazon*, which means more than just sight. It refers to divine revelation, a prophetic glimpse of what God intends to accomplish. This isn't wishful thinking or personal ambition dressed up in spiritual language. This is Heaven's blueprint being downloaded to Earth through surrendered hearts.

But here's what stops most of us: we've confused dreams with guarantees. We thought if God gave us the vision, the path would be straight and the timeline would be short. When detours came, when doors closed, and when others got what we were believing for, we assumed we heard wrong.

Sarah dreamed of motherhood for decades. Each month that passed felt like another nail in the coffin of hope. By the time Isaac was born, she was ninety years old—well past the age when dreams are supposed to come true. But God's timing isn't bound by human biology or social expectations. What looks impossible to us is simply another Tuesday for Him.

David was anointed as king while still a teenager, then spent years running from the current king who wanted him dead. The crown was promised, but the path to it led through caves, battles, and seasons of hiding. The dream didn't change—but David was transformed in the process of receiving it.

Joseph's dreams of leadership came through slavery and prison. Hannah's dream of a son came through years of barrenness and public humiliation.

Moses' dream of deliverance came through forty years of desert preparation.

The pattern is clear: God gives the vision, but He uses the waiting to prepare both you and the circumstances for its fulfillment.

So how do you know if it's time to resurrect a dream or release it?

Dreams from God have certain characteristics:

- They align with His character and Word
- They benefit others, not just yourself
- They grow stronger through opposition, not weaker
- They require God's power to accomplish
- They produce peace when you surrender the timeline to Him

Dreams from flesh tend to:

- Focus primarily on personal gain or recognition
- Demand immediate gratification
- Produce anxiety when delayed
- Rely solely on human effort and strategy
- Fade when circumstances get difficult

Maybe you've buried dreams under layers of disappointment. You've stopped talking about them because people got tired of hearing about "someday."

You've convinced yourself that contentment means settling for less than what God planted in your heart.

But what if the silence wasn't rejection? What if the delay was preparation? What if God was using the waiting to develop something in you that the dream requires—character, wisdom, compassion, and dependence on Him?

A woman I know dreamed of opening a nonprofit for homeless youth. For years, every door closed. Funding fell through. Partners backed out. She almost gave up—until she realized the delays had taught her things she needed to know. The failed attempts had connected her with the right people. The waiting had broken her of pride and taught her to depend on God's provision instead of her own fundraising ability. When the doors finally opened, she was ready not just with a vision, but with the maturity to steward it well.

Your dream may look different than you originally imagined. It may come later than you hoped. It may require more of you than you thought. But if it's from God, it will come.

Faith doesn't just believe God can resurrect the dead—it believes He can resurrect dreams that have been buried under years of disappointment.

Boldly Declare:

By faith, I can dream again.

Not because I'm naive, but because I serve a God who specializes in making the impossible inevitable. Not because I've figured out the timeline, but because I trust the One who holds it. Not because I understand the path, but because I know the destination is secure.

God, I give You the ashes of my broken expectations and receive the beauty of Your divine vision. I will not shrink my dreams to fit my circumstances. I will expand my faith to match Your promises.

The vision is for an appointed time. It will surely come.

By faith, I dream again.

Faith Moment

- Take out a piece of paper and write down one dream you've buried or stopped talking about. Don't analyze whether it's practical or possible—just write it down.
- Now ask God:
  - Is this vision still alive in Your heart for me?
  - What needs to change in me before it can manifest?
  - How do You want me to steward this dream during the waiting?
- Write your response: "God, I surrender my dream of … and I trust You to …"
- Declare this over your life: "By faith, I believe You are still working on what You promised. The delay is not denial. The silence is not rejection. I will dream again because You are the God of resurrection—and that includes resurrecting hope."

BY FAITH, YOU CAN

Acknowledgments

To the One who orders every step — my deepest gratitude belongs to God, who has carried me through seasons of doubt and delight, and whose faithfulness has never failed.

To my loved ones who have cheered, challenged, and covered me in prayer — thank you for holding me steady.

And to the quiet partner who walked beside me through every late night of writing, revision, and prayer — this book carries your fingerprints too. Our journey together is a reminder that faith and love can weave strength out of weakness, courage out of fear, and beauty out of the ordinary.

About the Author

Cassandra K. Faire-Cormier is a woman who understands that faith isn't just a Sunday word—it's a daily walk, through valleys and mountaintops alike. Her journey has been marked by seasons of deep questioning and moments of divine clarity, all woven together by an unwavering trust in God's faithfulness.

Through years of ministry, counseling, and personal experience, Cassandra has witnessed the transformative power of faith that refuses to quit. She has walked alongside individuals as they've navigated loss, disappointment, and breakthrough, always pointing them back to the One who never fails.

By Faith, I Can represents more than just her first published work—it's the culmination of lessons learned in the presence of God and refined through life's most challenging seasons.

When she's not writing or ministering, Cassandra enjoys early morning prayer walks, good coffee, and the deep conversations that happen around kitchen tables. Through this devotional, she hopes to encourage others to discover that faith isn't about having all the answers—it's about trusting the One who does.

Social media links

X   https://x.com/Faireing_Well

🅕   https://www.facebook.com/FaireingWell/

www.ingramcontent.com/pod-product-compliance
Lightning Source LLC
Chambersburg PA
CBHW032049040426
42449CB00007B/1039